Monday 2 November 2020

Attn: Rupert Sherbert Blank MP

Dear Rupert,

Thanks for taking the time to read this.

Covid 19. A virus now shown to be similar to the flu, with a similar mortality rate. 99.9% survivable by the majority. Only fatal to those with co-morbidities, with a high chance of pulling through, even then, given appropriate

treatment. Numbers comparable to other flu seasons, less than other pandemics.

Masks, social distancing, scientific censorship, offcom censorship, internet censorship, loneliness, mental illness, economic collapse, unemployment, virtually closed GPs, virtually closed dentists, abandonment by the legislature of its responsibilty, an executive governing by diktat, schools barely functioning, the undermining of policing by consent and the rule of law, a health service protected from use and discriminatory against the elderly (those most at risk and those who have personally paid most into said service), a timebomb backlog of cancelled NHS treatments, Lockdowns quarantining the well instead of the sick for the first time in history, a future level of debt unimaginable in peacetime.

Can you tell me your position on the Government reaction to Covid 19 and what risk assessments were undertaken?

Yours sincerely,

Dan

My MP did not reply. Here's Rupert!

Dearest, dearest Dan,

As a valued constituent, I felt I owed you a reply.

Firstly, - my, my, my! Who got out of bed on the wrong side, this morning? A little word to the wise, sleep is important. It may be tempting to try to run on only eight or nine hours a night but, trust me, it takes its toll. You sound stressed. Try to get at least eleven hours regularly and delegate properly. If you start your morning making your own breakfast, it'll be all downhill from there!

You've made a long list there. Really, an excellent example of a list. Superb.

Remember: Stay at home. Stay safe. Save lives.

That's my favourite list of all time.

The Government's position on Covid-19 (though what it's got to do with you, I don't know) is hiding behind the SAGE committee sofa.

I hope that helps, you darling child.

Yours sincerely,

Rupert Sherbert Blank MP

*P.S. SAVE THE NHS!!!! FOR GOD'S SAKE
SAVE THE NHS!!!!*

Wednesday 25 November 2020

Attn: Rupert Sherbert Blank MP

Wednesday 25 November 2020

Dear Rupert,

Thanks for taking the time to read this.

The UK's terrorism threat level has recently been raised to 'severe' after Islamic terrorist attacks in France, and elsewhere.

In light of the reasons for these attacks (the beheadings of innocents observing the 'wrong' faith or teaching the 'wrong' subjects) might it

not be a good idea for a cross-party declaration defending free speech as President Macron has done? Free speech being the cornerstone of Western civilisation and democracy.

We currently have a record number of muslim MPs.

Afzal Khan, Manchester Gorton

Rosena Allin-Khan, Tooting

Rupa Huq, Ealing Central & Acton

Tulip Siddiq, Hampstead & Kilburn

Mohammed Yasin, Bedford

Khalid Mahmood, Birmingham Perry Barr

Imran Hussein, Bradford East

Naz Shah, Bradford West

Shabana Mahmood, Birmingham Ladypool

Yasmin Qureshi, Bolton South East

Rushanara Ali, Bethnal Green & Bow

Tahir Ali, Birmingham Hall Green

Zarah Sultana,Coventry South

Apsana Begum,Poplar & Limehouse

Sajid Javid, Bromsgrove

Nusrat Ghani, Wealden

Rehman Chishti, Gillingham & Rainham

Saqib Bhatti,Meriden

Imran Ahmad Khan, Wakefield

If a declaration defending the values of free speech were to be headed by these MPs, then it would vividly demonstrate how the British culture of open enquiry, toleration of views and pursuit of critical thinking will allow anyone of ability to rise to the top of the country's law-making elite.

If lives are at stake, as they must be given the threat level, then it seems sensible to follow the French example.

I would appreciate your views on such a declaration.

Yours sincerely,

Dan

Shockingly, my MP did not reply. Here's Rupert!

Dear Dan,

Let me make it quite clear, I am terrified by by the increased level of terror implied by the increase in the terrorism level threat, and you should be too.

However, at least we don't live in France.

Free speech is all very well and I support it. However, speech that causes offense is hate speech, not free speech. I am all for speech that I agree with but speech that upsets me is illegal. In my book, questioning my expenses, or my morals, or my religion is out of bounds, Praise Allah.

As a devout Christian, I can tell you that our history is chock-a-block with beheadings. Have you heard of the Spanish Inquisition or Henry the Eighth? I would keep your head down if I were you (I'm not suggesting that humorously. Humour is very often hate speech, of course, and I would not be a party to that).

The cornerstone of Western Democracy is now Covid-19, for your information.

When you say 'allow anyone of ability to rise to the top of the country's law-making elite' what you really mean is even muslims. No-one should be grateful to the society that allows them to get to the top. They got there despite society. And so did I.

I cannot quite understand why you think our muslim MP's should stand up for British values, though. Haven't they been through enough? Why should they be singled out? Have you got some kind of a problem? Are you a racist?

Kindest regards,

Rupert Sherbert Blank MP

Wednesday 2 December 2020

Attn: Rupert Sherbert Blank MP

Dear Rupert,

Thanks for taking the time to read this.

In light of your vote for the new coronavirus restrictions on 1/12/20, can you tell me how you responded to the briefing paper submitted to MPs on 29/11/20 by Clare Craig BM BCh FRCPath, Jonathan Engler MBChB LLB, Mike Yeadon BSc Hons (Biochem-tox) PhD

(Pharmacol) and Christian McNeill LL.B and Dip LP?

This paper states that: PCR-testing is unfit for mass implementation. Testing those without symptoms is a nonsense. The false-positive rate is so high as to be creating a pseudo-epidemic. The definition of COVID deaths is too broad. Not all excess deaths are COVID related. Unnecessary self-isolation is leading to a NHS staffing crisis. The only confirmatory testing in Liverpool, using the Lateral Flow Test, has shown no Covid. The LFT is a far superior test, which is highlighting the failure of PCR. The results of PCR testing do not fit reality on the ground.

A lockdown based on testing is not needed and actually makes the situation worse.

Can you also point me towards the evidence you did use to inform your vote, so that I can better understand your decision?

Yours sincerely,

Dan

THIS IS THE ACTUAL REPLY, WITH RUPERT SUBSTITUTED FOR MY MP'S REAL NAME.

Dear Dan,

Thank you very much for your email.

I am afraid I am unaware of this briefing submitted by Ms Craig and Mr Engler so am unaware of their findings or recommendations.

When voting yesterday, I based my decision on the arguments put forward by the Government and various MPs.

While I agree the tiered system is not perfect, it is a workable solution that allows people to clearly understand restrictions in their area.

I am happy to take a look at the briefing you mention if you have a copy of it, and will pass them on to my ministerial colleagues.

With kind regards,

Rupert

MY REACTION

Well.....I got a reply, at least.

Rupert isn't aware of the briefing. Well, can't read everything, I suppose. And he'll pass it on. That's good, I suppose.

When voting, he based his decision on the arguments put forward by the Government and various MPs. Ah.

No mention of evidence. For a lockdown of the healthy that destroys the country and has no evidence of it's own to endorse it. Not too good, Rupert.

And nobody clearly understood the tier system. Not even on a good day. Not even on the first day.

Rupert gets 2 out of 10. 1 for answering and 1 for passing on the evidence that he did not know about but I did. Which one of us was voting again?

Tuesday 8 December 2020

Attn: Rupert Sherbert Blank MP

Dear Rupert,

Thanks for taking the time to read this.

Re: E-petition 323442. Prevent any restrictions on those who refuse a Covid-19 vaccination. Parliamentary briefing on Monday 14, December 2020.

Please can I ask that you consider adding your weight to supporting the above petition in the upcoming session?

In a public document (Reg 174 Information for UK Healthcare Professionals), published before the vaccine rollout, it states that 'It is unknown whether Covid-19 mRNA Vaccine BNT162b2 has an impact on fertility.'

The vaccine has been produced in record time. You might almost say rushed.

The companies involved have been given a legal indemnity, protecting them from being sued.

NHS staff are also protected from legal action arising from mis-management of the vaccine.

At the height of the pandemic, between the 1st of March and the 30th of June, the ONS reports that of the deaths involving Covid-19 in England and Wales, 91.1% had at least one pre-existing condition. The survival rate overall for the population was over 99%. There is no valid reason to compel people to take a vaccine that presents so low a threat.

The experience of human experimentation during World War Two shows the importance of a human being having the right to ultimate control over his or her own body.

The experience of Thalidomide shows the importance of a human being having the right to ultimate control over his or her health. No-one should be sanctioned for exercising that right.

Yours sincerely,

Dan

MY MP'S ACTUAL REPLY

Dear Dan,

Thank you very much for your email.

I understand that there are no plans by the UK Government to make vaccination compulsory and those who do not wish to be vaccinated do not have to.

The Pfizer vaccine has been trialled by over 40,000 people, which has allowed the vaccine to be deployed faster than ordinary trials, which often take longer due to a lack of volunteers.

There are exemptions for people who are ill or pregnant already to mitigate the risk as was demonstrated during the Thalidomide disaster.

I have been reassured that the vaccine is safe and look forward to receiving my own when the time is right.

With kind regards,

Rupert.

MY REACTION

Elllo Rupert! Despite how underwhelming the replies have been so far, it is good to get one.

Straightaway, I notice that Rupert has tacitly declined to add his weight to anything.

The vaccine has been trialled (tested on) by 40000 people. Over 10 months. Just look up testing for all other vaccines and tell me if you think that's enough. It might be safe, I can concede that. But it's a guess, isn't it? And we all have to have it, not just the vulnerable.

Theoretically, there is an exemption for everyone who does not want to take the vaccine. But we all know about the societal pressure being exerted here. Is there a chance of infertility for the young who take it? Or worse? Have you heard anyone staking their reputation on saying there isn't?

And, big sigh.......Covid 19 isn't all that dangerous to the already healthy.

So, Mr Blank. You get a 1 out of 10 for replying

Saturday 9th January 2021

Attn: Rupert Sherbert Blank MP

Saturday 9 January 2021

Dear Rupert,

Thanks for taking the time to read this.

It's time for our elected MPs to make a case for the equation COVID-19 = PLAGUE. Only a contagious threat on the level of the black death can justify the Government's present policy. However, a threat on that level would not need Government coercion, would it? Statutory instruments would be irrelevant before the threat. We would all hide in our houses out of common sense.

The lack of proportion is staggering.

Sir Edward Leigh MP of your own party asked the Prime Minister how the public can be asked to endure a third lockdown in light of the fact that less than 400 people under 60 have died from the virus. Out of a population of 60 million plus.

The Prime Minister did not address the numbers.

The lack of proportion is staggering.

In **********, there have been 9 deaths from COVID since last March.From a population 0f 11000. That's a 0.09% death rate. In ************, there has been 1 death from COVID since last March. From a population of 18000. That;s a 0.006% death rate.

I am largely unable to leave my house based on these numbers.

I am unable to visit my family in ********* based on these numbers.

The numbers are taken from the ONS

(https://www.ons.gov.uk/peoplepopulationandc ommunity/healthandsocialcare/causesofdeath /articles/deathsinvolvingcovid19interactivemap /2020-06-12).

The lack of proportion is staggering.

You're my elected MP. I voted for you. You need to tell people like me why I should be frightened of COVID-19.

You need to correct my maths (should be easy) and show me where the plague is. Not tests, not cases, not models, but the deadly COVID-19.

Then check out this website, https://www.victimsoflockdown.com/, and show me that it is proportionate.

Yours sincerely,

Dan

THIS IS THE ACTUAL REPLY, WITH RUPERT SUBSTITUTED FOR MY MP'S REAL NAME.

Dear Dan,

Thank you for your email regarding the latest national lockdown.

*I am pleased that in ************** the number of cases have been generally low, with only a few serious outbreaks in places such as ***********.*

However what we have seen over the Christmas period and into the new year is the number of cases remaining at a very high rate, and the death rate continuing to be quite alarming.

The primary reason for introducing further lockdown measures is to one, reduce the rate of infection so that the R rate drops below 1, meaning the spread of the virus is shrinking instead of growing.

The second reason is that of NHS capacity. As I am sure you are all too aware, hospitals right across the UK have been near maximum capacity and without introducing restrictions there is a very real fear that this would spill over capacity.

As MP, I could not in good conscious vote to remove lockdown restrictions when hospitals are near capacity and lives would be at risk.

I understand the frustration felt by many, including myself, at the nature of lockdowns and the disruption they have caused to our lives. However with the rapid rollout of the vaccine, and death and new infection instances falling, I remain hopeful that the worst of the virus is behind us and things can begin to return to normal.

Thank you once again for writing to me. I hope this helps explain my views and the logic for introducing lockdowns.

With kind regards,

Rupert

MY REACTION

Rupert replied! Or was it a cut and paste job?

No mention of excess deaths. None. All cases, all R rates.

NHS capacity trotted out, without context. It's winter. ICUs are always full but that does not mean overrun, rather it is best practice to maximise their usefulness. Capacity is dependent on staff, who are self-isolating (asymptomatically, mostly, with an illness that is over 99% survivable). The Nightingale Hospitals were never used.

In the same letter, Rupert says deaths are falling and infections are down! Sort of undermines his logic, which his letter hasn't explained at all.

Rupert, like the Prime Minister, left the numbers that I stated alone and did not balance the Plague equation.

Sorry, old boy! 1 out of 10. You managed to answer.

Tuesday 19th January 2021

Att: Rupert Sherbert Blank MP

Dear Rupert,

Thanks for taking the time to read this letter.

As I understand it, the requirement for mask mandates has to be reviewed by the Secretary of State before the end of the period six months after they came into force. They came into force on July 24th 2020 (well after the pandemic peak), so need to be reviewed by January 23rd 2021.

40 years of study have not produced definite conclusions about the benefits of masks, even those used by surgeons in operations. Scientific authorities (Fauci, WHO et al) all pronounced them unnecessary at the start of the COVID 19 crisis, based on those 40 years of study. The only study during the crisis, The Danish Mask Study, found there were no benefits to wearing masks. Then, of course, there is a wide difference in the quality of masks used. The study used "high-quality surgical masks with a filtration rate of 98%". I doubt this is the case with the vast majority of the general public.

https://swprs.org/danish-mask-study-no-benefit/

https://www.acpjournals.org/doi/10.7326/M20-6817

Please stop the compulsory wearing of masks. They cause social division, have unknown consequences for dental and respiratory health, are mentally corrosive for the young and old alike (it is an inherent part of our society to see and respond to facial cues) and invite a cultural OCD that weakens the ability of all to take the risks needed to assure our quality of life.

Locking the people in their homes is wrong. The compulsory wearing of masks when they dare venture out is the cruelty of twisting the knife. Please at least stop that cruelty.

Yours sincerely,

Dan

My MP did not reply. Here's Rupert!

Dear Dan,

Thank you so much for your letter.

I'm afraid it has made me rather emotional. I will never, ever give up masks! Never!

As I read your hilariously neurotic correspondence, I laugh under my mask, and nobody knows. I stick my tongue out at old ladies, and nobody knows. I leer at young girls, and nobody knows. I dribble, burp and grin, and nobody knows.

Masks are the greatest!

And you want to take that away from me? Over 40 years of study has shown that politicians don't give back powers that they have been given. Y'know the old joke - how do you tell if a politician is lying? Now you can't see my lips moving, one way or the other! This is paradise!

Masks with a filtration rate of 98% are easy to come by.   Just depends on what you want to filter. Mine filters 98% of human interaction with constituents....so get used to the new normal because I'm never giving that up!

Cultural OCD? I bet you felt very clever when you thought that up. Like we did when we thought up Covid.

I'm not mocking you. Under this mask, I'm wearing a caring, understanding, nurturing expression.

Honest.

Yours sincerely,

Rupert Sherbert Blank MP

Tuesday 9 February 2021

Attn: Rupert Sherbert Blank MP

Dear Rupert,

Thanks for taking the time to read this.

I am writing because our country is sliding towards a permanent state of lockdown. This, in itself, is a dire state of affairs. Within it, though, is something worse. I believe in the two party system of representative government. This, as you know, places my elected representative between me and my government. This gives me a stake in my country and provides my government a mandate based on my consent to be governed through this system.

At present, my elected representative (as in every other constituency) is missing in action: i.e. the legislature is inactive. There is no real reason to lobby my MP regarding the proposed lawmaking of the executive when my MP is not afforded the opportunity of voting on any proposed legislation. This not only removes my MP, it also removes me.

There are only a few short steps between this state of affairs and a rescinding of the consent to be governed. The late Sir Roger Scuton said, 'Without freedom there cannot be government by consent; and it is the freedom to participate in the process of government, and to protest against, dissent from, and oppose the decisions that are made in my name, that confer on me the dignity of citizenship.'

The dignity of citizenship is exactly what is being denied us.

A case-in-point has recently been raised by Dr John Fanning, Senior Lecturer in Tort law at the University of Liverpool. He states that Schedule 21 of the 2020 Coronavirus Act contains powers that the state can deploy against "potentially infectious persons".

'This means that a person who refused to submit to a doorstep test could potentially be arrested, taken to a suitable facility, and required by law to undergo COVID-19 testing. The imagery this evokes is utterly chilling; the Coronavirus Act is like a dystopian fantasy in statutory form. There are few laws on the books that can rival it.'

These are the Doctor's words.

My MP needs to be between me and legislation like this.

Scruton added, 'The difference between the West and the rest is that Western societies are governed by politics; the rest are ruled by power.'

Which catagory does the Coronavirus 2020 Act fall into?

Yours sincerely,

Dan

My MP Replied

Dear Dan,

Thank you very much for your email regarding the current lockdown situation and the concerns you have about democratic oversight.

I should start off by saying that the House of Commons is not inactive and members are still partaking in the legislative process with hybrid proceedings in Parliament.

I have had the pleasure to speak in various debates during this latest lockdown and am still able to vote for or against matters in the House.

For example this Thursday I hope to speak in the General Debate on Wales which is an annual event which coincides with St David's Day, which continues undeterred.

Of course, in Wales coronavirus regulations are decided by the Senedd, which still sits and discuses their laws and motions, committees still sit and the business of Government has continued despite the restrictions that affect our lives.

I hope you share my optimism that the UK Government have announced a roadmap out of lockdown and the Devolved Authorities have also announced steps they are taking to exit lockdowns.

While these times are difficult for us all, the light is at the end of the tunnel and I look forward for this being behind us.

With kind regards,

Rupert

MY REACTION

This was like a bad passport photo - my letter makes me cringe. But I meant it.

Rupert didn't seem to take it seriously. He's speaking in debates. Ace! He's voting! Ace! But on what? Nothing of consequense, or he would have brought them up instead of the General Debate on Wales, which looks like an excuse to pig out on bara-brith. It continues undeterred!

But Wales handles its own crap, so don't blame me.

Rupert - all the new regulations are bumped through via statutory orders off of the 1984

Health Act, precisely so they can't be held up by the legislative process, and to avoid a periodic review that could end them.

You get 1 point for replying and get it deducted for being a crippling coward stuck in the wrong job - a job you're destroying, along with your country. Sorry, old chap, for coming down so hard, but you took the specifics of my crummy letter and flushed 'em rather than answering them.

Friday 12 March 2021

Attn: Rupert Sherbert Blank MP

Dear Rupert,

Thanks for taking the time to read this.

On Monday 15th of March, MPs will be debating vaccine passports in response to an internet petition.

In December of last year, you responded to my concerns over compulsory vaccinations and stated that the UK Government had no plans for this.

Vaccine passports are clearly a way for our government to outsource responsibility for mandating vaccinations.

Since the imposition of lockdown last year, the UK government has slavishly followed the playbook of the CCP.

On Wednesday, the Chinese dictatorship (which first covered up Covid-19 and then exported it to the world, incurring no penalty except being the only country to increase its GDP in 2020) launched its domestic vaccine passport and has urged the WHO to let it build and run a global database.

This is social credit scoring.

Bad enough to have it in a country that abuses it's citizens, mentally and physically. But do we want it here, in free, democratic society? It's getting harder and harder to make the distinction between the two nations. I am still under lockdown - no-one in Wuhan is.

The survival rate from Covid-19 is over 99% overall.

The average age of death from Covid-19 is 84. UK life expectancy is 81.

Please go to the debate and tell them that we are not China. If you can't do that, why not?

Yours sincerely,

Dan

MY MP REPLIED

Dear Dan,

Thank you for contacting me about vaccine passports, or COVID status certification.

I am incredibly proud of the progress that the UK is making in vaccinating the population, with one in three adults receiving their first dose, and I am delighted that the Government reached the goal of offering a vaccine to priority groups 1-4, over 15 million people, by 15 February.

While I understand that a range of options are being considered to encourage people to receive the vaccine, the Government does not plan to make the COVID-19 vaccination mandatory.

As set out in the Government's Roadmap towards easing restrictions, four programmes of work have been established to consider different aspects of how the UK should handle COVID-19 from summer onwards. One of these is a review into whether COVID-status certification could play a role in reopening our economy, reducing restrictions on social contact and improving safety.

Of course, COVID-status certificates raise complex ethical and discriminatory issues that would need to be worked through.

This is something I know the Government and the Prime Minister are conscious of and I welcome the fact that the Government is considering these issues fully as part of the review.

I have noted the concerns you have raised, which I will ensure ministers are made aware of throughout the review process.

It is right that we rule out no options at this stage.

Conclusions and the outcome of the review will be set out in advance of Step four of the Roadmap.

As the Prime Minister has said, it may be that there is a role for certification in the future, but for now the emphasis is rightly on our vaccination and testing programmes.

Thank you again for taking the time to contact me.

Best wishes, Rupert

My Reaction

Rupert got back to me. That's 1 point, right there.

It's also fair to say that he's replying fairly regularly. That's another point.

I'm on a roll now. It's nice being nice to Rupert! He also said that he'll pass on my concerns during the review. I believe him!
"Fellas......there's this guy, and he thinks...." I could turn this whole thing around! Another point for Rupert Sherbert Blank MP.

But, he's peaked at 3 points.

My major concern was that the Government would leave discrimination to the private sector, ensuring that requiring passports/certificates would mean requiring vaccines: a mandate by the back door. Rupert didn't address this.

You'd think, given that my letter got a little snarky, that Rupert would have rebutted the China comparison. Nope. He's above that.

As usual, the figures relating to Covid - which do not seem scary to me - frighten the dickens out of Rupert. They are so terrifying that he won't even mention them. I wonder when he will?

Telling me that 'the Government does not plan to make the COVID-19 vaccination mandatory' made me feel warm inside. Sadly, a paragraph or two down, he tells me that 'It is right that we rule out no options at this stage.' I think there are plenty of options we should rule out.

'As the Prime Minister has said, it may be that there is a role for certification in the future'

How about we rule that out, chump?

3 Out of 10.   Sorry for calling you a chump.

Friday 19th March 2021

Dear Rupert,

Thanks for taking the time to read this.

Ahead of the upcoming vote in Parliament to renew the Coronavirus Act, I'm hopeful that you will consider downloading and reading the new report (pub. 18th March 2021) from the Health Advisory and Recovery Team (HART). It can be found here: https://www.hartgroup.org/covid-19-evidence/

The only evidence considered by our lawmakers is that supplied by the members of SAGE. I think that the qualifications of the members of HART are equally eminent, much like the signatories of the Great Barrington Declaration: https://gbdeclaration.org/

It's hard to understand why these experts are sidelined from the debate, although there is not much of a debate.

Anyway - I hope this information is useful.

Yours sincerely,

Dan

NO REPLY - HERE'S WHAT I IMAGINE IT MIGHT HAVE BEEN

Dear Dan,

You sound depressed, defeated and paralysed by the magnitude of the problems facing you.

And they said all political lives end in failure!

Since your letter was short, I'll return the favour and thank you kindly for the enclosed information. We now know where to go to round up the troublemakers.

Kidding!

Yours ingratiatingly,

Rupert.

P.S. I trust the home address you have supplied is correct. Just so we know.

Wednesday 24 March 2021

Dear Rupert,

Thanks for reading this. I am writing to express my concern about the Coronavirus Act renewal motion.

A year after this emergency Act was passed, I am urging you to repeal the Coronavirus Act on 25th March, to protect rights and justice in the UK. The Coronavirus Act represents the biggest expansion of executive power in a generation.

Some of the powers in the Act are extreme, unexplained and simply unjustified — but, nodded through on the premise of urgency, the Act suffered from a lack of parliamentary scrutiny.

It is vital that this motion to review the Act is not a rubber-stamping exercise but a genuine review and repeal of the Act's unnecessary and dangerous powers.

The most dangerous and excessive of these powers are Schedules 21 and 22 of the Act.

Schedule 21 contains some of the most extreme detention powers in modern British legal history. It gives unprecedented, almost arbitrary powers to the police, immigration officers and public health officials to detain "potentially infectious" members of the public, including children, potentially indefinitely and in unspecified locations. In a pandemic, that could mean anyone.

Schedule 21 detention powers have been used for 252 prosecutions — every single one of which was found unlawful by the CPS on review. This 100% unlawful prosecution rate, which has continued month after month over the past year, is unprecedented and unacceptable.

Big Brother Watch has found cases of innocent and healthy individuals not only being arrested and fined but even held in police cells unlawfully under these draconian powers.

Renewing Schedule 21 in the Coronavirus Act would be dangerous and indefensible. Significant powers in the Health and Social Care Act 2008 already allow for the forced detention and testing of potentially infectious people with the authorisation of a magistrate, which is a vital safeguard.

Furthermore, the Health Protection (Coronavirus, Restrictions) (Self-Isolation) Regulations 2020 require individuals who test positive to self-isolate and give police the power to forcibly return an individual to an isolation place.

Schedule 22 gives the Secretary of State extraordinary powers to prohibit gatherings, meaning protests, vigils and political assemblies could be banned at ministerial discretion.

Schedule 22 has never been activated in England and so is plainly unnecessary, but neither is it proportionate in a democracy. All the time it sits on the statute books it poses a threat to the right to free expression, freedom of assembly and democracy.

Please vote to repeal these dangerous powers on 25th March.

Yours sincerely,
Dan.

MY MP REPLIED

Dear Dan,

Thank you very much for your email regarding the Coronavirus Act, and raising your concerns with me.

The Act, like all Acts of Parliament, is subject to Parliamentary scrutiny, and I believe the Act receives the scrutiny it needs both in the House of Commons and in Parliamentary Select Committees.

I do understand the concern felt about executive power, the likes of which we have not seen since the Second World War. However these are exceptional circumstances and regrettably the Government have had to introduce rules that while unpopular, have contributed towards saving lives.

I completely appreciate your concerns about the power conferred by the Coronavirus Act relating to people who may be infectious.
I know that most people have been working extremely hard, and making numerous sacrifices, to comply with relevant public health advice.

This provision simply seeks to ensure that isolation measures can be enforced if necessary.

In practice, this power would take the form of a public health officer or police officer returning people to places that they have been required to stay. For example, if someone has been contacted by NHS Test and Trace and required to self-isolate for 14 days, and then is found out and about during that time, they would be returned home.

Equally, the Act empowers police and immigration officers to make sure that individuals attend testing or treatment facilities as required.

I understand that these measures may seem intimidating, and I know that the overwhelming majority of people are following guidance and obeying self-isolation instructions. However, we must be prepared to enforce these measures, to ensure that the small number of people who do not comply are not putting lives at risk by their behaviour.

Thank you once again for taking the time to write to me. The Act is up for review again before the summer recess where it is hoped that by the final phases of lifting of lockdown in England on June 21st will mean that Act will no longer be required and will be subsequently repealed.

With kind regards,

Rupert.

MY REACTION

It'd be nice to click my heels together and break open the champagne instead of lighting the pilot on the gas oven and shoving my head in.....

How are executive powers not seen since WWII proportional to a virus that (deep breath, mantra) is well Over 99% survivable and kills, sadly but not surprisingly, those of an average age of 84 - WHO ARE ALREADY SICK! Sorry for shouting.

How has locking up the healthy saved lives?

Half of the dead were in care homes. With DNR instructions taped to their chests. Meanwhile the CDC and NHS reports that deaths because of heart disease and cancer dwarf COVID-19 in 2020.

'People who may be infectious.' You said a mouthful there. Or may not be ....

'Numerous sacrifices.' Jesus Christ man, get your head out of your ass and look at those sacrifices.

'The Act empowers police and immigration officers to make sure that individuals attend testing or treatment facilities as required.' And how impressive have the actions of the police been during the last year? How well has the law been implemented on the ground? No-one can argue that there isn't entertainment value in watching masked men (police) marching old ladies away from dangerous park benches and into safe police vans, but the fun can't go on forever. Maybe with the Coronavirus Act, though, it can.

'We must be prepared to enforce these measures, to ensure that the small number of people who do not comply are not putting lives at risk by their behaviour.' In other words, it's for your own good: the excuse used by every communist tyrant.   I put more lives at risk just driving my car to the shops. Seriously, I'm a terrible driver, I can't tell you how many people I've killed - but it's all good: each and every one had a positive Covid test less than 28 days before, so I'm in the clear.

0 out of 10, Rupert. 0 out of 10.

Monday 19 April 2021

Dear Rupert,

Thanks for taking the time to read this.

This month, an open letter from Christian Leaders (1352 signatories) was delivered to the Prime Minister. Hopefully, you have had a chance to read it, as it details the terrible lack of ethical consideration given to the revolting idea of a COVID passport/certificate.

There are three main points covered.

Here, in their own words:

'Firstly, to make vaccination the basis of whether someone is allowed entry to a venue, or participation in an activity, makes no logical sense in terms of protecting others. If the vaccines are highly effective in preventing significant disease, as seems to be the evidence from trial results to date, then those who have been vaccinated have already received protection; there is no benefit to them from other people being vaccinated. Further, since vaccines do not prevent infection per se even a vaccinated person could in theory carry and potentially pass on the virus, so to decide someone's "safe non-spreader" status on the basis of proof of their immunity to disease is spurious.

Secondly, the introduction of vaccine passports would constitute an unethical form of coercion and violation of the principle of informed consent. We risk creating a two-tier society, a medical apartheid in which an underclass of people who decline vaccination are excluded from significant areas of public life. There is also a legitimate fear that this scheme would be the thin end of the wedge leading to a permanent state of affairs in which COVID vaccine status could be expanded to encompass other forms of medical treatment and perhaps even other criteria beyond that. This scheme has the potential to bring about the end of liberal democracy as we know it and to create a surveillance state in which the government uses technology to control certain aspects of citizens' lives. As such, this constitutes one of the most dangerous policy proposals ever to be made in the history of British politics.

Finally, as Christian leaders we wish to state that we envisage no circumstances in which we could close our doors to those who do not have a vaccine passport, negative test certificate, or any other "proof of health". For the Church of Jesus Christ to shut out those deemed by the state to be social undesirables would be anathema to us.'

Regardless of the fact that COVID-19 vaccines fall foul of the Nuremberg Code (they are still experimental), regardless of the immunity from liability enjoyed by the manufacturers, and regardless of the fact that COVID-19 is hardly life threatening for most people, the government has still felt the need to press ahead with this. Informed consent, equality under the law and freedom of association are all under threat from this quasi-communist, quasi-technocratic development. Please speak out against it.

As a side note, I would add that I am not a Christian. At this moment, voting Conservative is also beginning to look like a dubious act of faith to me.

Yours sincerely,
Dan.

MY MP DID NOT REPLY. HERE'S WHAT RUPERT THINKS

Dear Dan......dear God Dan,

Christians!   Is that where we're at now?

All they have are morals and ethical lessons to live a better life. No facts, no figures. Just superstitious rubbish.

There's nothing superstitious about masks. Or social distancing. Or lockdowns.   Or vaccines. They are based on cold, hard facts which I can't find for you right now.

Do you like it when the God-Squad knock at your door? Course you don't, so don't expect me to. What have Christians ever done for us anyway? All those weird rituals.

Please cheer up. We are, after all, now allowing you to hug, provided you wear a mask and do not do it face-to-face (in anticipation of your next letter, I don't know either. It's the government guidance, so bloody well do it!!!!)

Love and virtual kisses,

Your Obediant Overlord,

Rupert

P.S. I really love how worried these bible thumpers are about creating a two-tier society. That's really funny when you think about it. It's like being worried about finding jam in a doughnut.

MY MP DID ACTUALLY REPLY AFTER A LOOOOONG TIME.

Dear Daniel,

Thank you for contacting me about vaccine passports, or COVID status certification.

Please accept my apologies for the delay in getting back to you.

I have had the opportunity to speak to my colleagues in Government about the proposals. I am sure, like me, we can be incredibly proud of the progress that the UK is making in vaccinating the population and I am delighted that the Government reached, ahead of schedule, the goal of offering a vaccine to priority groups 1-9, by 15 April. This means that all adults over 50, the clinically vulnerable and health and social care workers have now been offered a life-saving COVID-19 vaccine.

While supply continues to be the rate limiting factor and the rollout is not without its challenges, the Government remains on track to offer first doses of the vaccine to all adults by the end of July.

I believe that as the UK opens up to International travel and other nations ask for proof of vaccination for entry into their country, that the UK Government considers an easy way to streamline this process and make it easier for individuals to prove their vaccine status. I believe that for international travel they may be necessary.

However, I have raised concerns about the proposals domestically and the UK Government have decided not to introduce these proposals. I was concerned about creating a tiered system of those who were vaccinated and those who were not yet vaccinated, as well as putting additional pressure on establishments to screen for these certifications also, as many businesses are already following strict social distancing and public health guidance in order to be able to trade.

I hope this information is helpful. Thank you again for taking the time to contact me.

With kind regards,
Rupert.

Monday 26 April 2021

Dear Rupert,

Thanks for taking the time to read this letter.

I have a simple question, the answer to which should be common knowledge.

How safe do we need to be from Covid before we can go back to normal?

If we are following science, this is a question that must be answered since science must be falsifiable.

Actually, it was answered once. In the Government's original Pandemic Preparedness Strategy.
(https://www.theguardian.com/world/ng-interactive/2020/feb/27/what-are-the-uks-plans-for-dealing-with-a-pandemic-virus)

We know that a death toll of up to 315,000 within a few months from a pandemic virus was envisaged as being acceptable – still far more than we have seen with the (PCR-inflated) Covid death toll of the past year. That scale of mortality was not deemed to warrant any of the unprecedented measures we have experienced since March 2020.

There is the question of why these preparations were abandoned but, rather than argue over a dead dog, would it be possible to have some concrete scientific criteria specifying when this will be officially over: i.e. when is a pandemic not a pandemic, according to science?

N.B. One incontestable fact of the pandemic: the average age of death from COVID is higher than overall UK life expectancy. Perhaps this would be a useful scientific measure?

Yours sincerely,
Dan

NO REPLY. TRY THIS.

Dear Dan,

Now, I'm sorry, but you've started making things up.

A Pandemic What Plan? Never heard of it! And your source is The Guardian! Who told them these silly things?

The pandemic is over when we say it is over! When no-one is dying! When everybody is safe!

Oh, you evil man!

One of my constituents has recently died of Covid, and after suffering so much already with obesity and diabetes, heart disease and chronic pulmonary obstructive disease. Crashing his motorcycle on the way home from his 95th birthday celebration at Macdonalds was the last straw!

Actually, Covid was.

And my dog is dead. And yes. It was Covid.

Stay safe. Save lives. Live long and prosper. May The Force Be With You.

Love you, Rupert.

Tuesday 11 May 2021

Dear Rupert,

Thanks for taking the time to read this.

Does morality and ethics have any part to play in government policy?

Does it matter, or are there more pragmatic considerations to be considered?

I think vaccinating children with an experimental (testing does not finish until 2023) product to protect an at-risk group of an average age of 82-84 is immoral.

I think the suppression of a cheap, viable prevention and cure for Covid (Ivermectin), as well as information about the health benefits of zinc, vitamin D and C is immoral.

I think a state-run campaign to instil fear in it's citizens to protect sick, elderly citizens who are as likely to die from the flu as from Covid is immoral.

Locking up the well to protect the sick is immoral.

Creating a huge national debt to 'safeguard' the sick elderly is immoral.

Censoring debate over Covid is immoral.

Vaccine Passports are immoral.

A Freedom of Information request has recently confirmed that zero prosecutions have been made under the Coronavirus Act. The Crown Prosecution Service stated that all offences charged under the act were incorrectly charged. How many fines have been paid for not breaking the law? The entire Coronavirus Act is an immoral enterprise and it should be repealed.

I could go on and on (it probably feels like I go on and on) about the endless immorality of recent times, from the sheer gall (and immorality) of the state thinking it has a right to dictate when we can hug one another, to the Covid-Only NHS.

For reference, I include the Oxford English Dictionary definition of immorality. It is 'not conforming to accepted standards of morality.' What is the government's standard of morality? Can you defend it? If not, why should I accept it?

Yours sincerely,
Dan

NO REPLY FROM RUPERT. HERE'S WHAT I THINK HE'LL SAY.

Dear Dan,
You do go on and on. There, I said it!!!! Bet it's not the first time you've heard it.
Ethics and morality have their place, of course, but are you whiter than white? I mean, you're really on my case, old chap. No-one, however, is shining the spotlight on you. I'm sending a

freedom of information request your way, you lucky man: tell me, what is your problem? Please reply in under a thousand words and include illustrations for any sexual inadequances or perversions.

We need to get to the bottom of this!

If we don't tell you when to hug, sir, who does? Who makes the rules if we don't? Don't you believe in rules of any kind? I expect you walk on the grass that has the 'Don't walk on the grass' sign. You're not coming round my house, mate!

We have to get these kids injected to save granny. Where are your morals? How many dead grannies are enough for you? Picture them lying end to end. They'd probably go a long way. I think I've made my point.

Look up the word 'self-righteous' in the Oxford English Dictionary. Your picture will be under it.

BOOM!

With love and affection,

Rupert Sherbert Blank MP

Monday 31 May 2021

Dear Rupert,

Thanks for taking the time to read this.

On the 27th May 2021, the Recovery Campaign delivered a copy of Laura Dodsworth's new book, 'A State of Fear', to all 650 MPs.

I think all MPs should read it.

The use of behavioural science, nudge theory and branches of the armed services (Brigade 77) to instil fear in the British people is a sick new development, new to national life.

Frighteningly similar to the methods of the CCP, these methods show contempt for the people.

The BBC (TV and radio), ITV, Channel 4, national newspapers etc have all followed a rigid line of catastrophizing propaganda, with vanishingly few alternative viewpoints (and even those are comprehensively rubbished).

Government announcements are strictly worse-case scenarios, and those are never re-visited when they are (almost invariably) proved wrong.

Positive developments are never addressed (unless in the cause of untested vaccine promotion).

Scientific enquiry only exists within the boundaries of promoting government policy. So not scientific at all.

Cost/benefit analysis' are a thing of the past. As is a sensible evaluation of risk.

This is a disaster for the country and its people. It's a disaster that's going to reach far into the future and blight the lives of our kids and their kids. Please read the book.

Yours sincerely,
Dan.

Rupert did not reply. Here's What I think He Wants to Write

Dear God Dan,
I must respectfully remind you that I was not elected to read books. By the way, what does CCP stand for?

Yours sincerely,

Rupert.

Sunday 13 June 2021

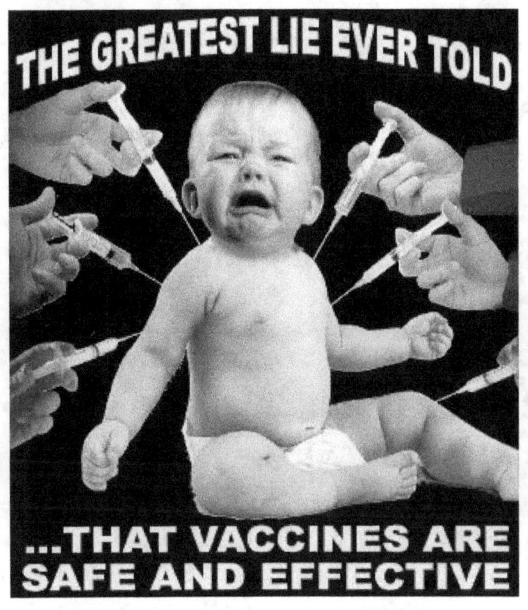

Dear Rupert,

Thanks for reading this.

It's unbelievable that anyone should want to encourage children to be vaccinated for Covid-19, and that anyone should have to write a letter to those in authority to argue against such a move.

However, I find myself doing so.

The chances of a child dying from Covid are statistically zero. If you can't argue for vaccination on the basis of the health of the individual vaccinated, then you cannot argue for it.

The children that die from these 'emergency' vaccines (please quantify the 'emergency' facing these kids) will have been wantonly sacrificed by doctors, nurses, politicians and parents. Those who physically perform the act of vaccinations, and who are paid a bonus to do so in each case, are guilty of, at least, manslaughter when a fatality occurs. It is not extreme to say this when First Do No Harm becomes Take This Even Though You Don't Need It.

Ethical doctors know this. Over 40 of them have written an open letter to the MHRA (Medicine and

Health Products Regulatory Agency), for a second time insisting that these plans are stopped. You can find their first letter here: https://www.hartgroup.org/open-letter-child-vaccination/

The MHRA have also received a letter from Evidence-based Medicine Consultancy Ltd, which urges the suspension of all vaccinations based on their preliminary study of the Yellow Card reporting system. They found that between 4th January 2021 and 26th May 2021 there have been 1253 Covid Vaccine-attributed deaths and 888,196 adverse drug reactions. You can find their letter here: https://www.e-bmc.co.uk/

Anyone who ignores this, and has the power to stop it, is culpable.

Yours sincerely,
Dan

Welllll....Rupert's too busy for this hot potato. Here's what he might have said.

Dear Dan,

I am trying to hold my temper. Do you believe me to be a danger to young children?

I only want to help them. That's why I got into politics.   It's all about the children. I believe the children are our future.

That's got a ring to it. (Note to self - put that to music and propose an all-party parliamentary group on the subject. Rupert Blank and the All-Party Parliamentary Group…..now, there's a band!)

Listen, citizen, you expect far too much from your elected representatives. I can't just wave a magic wand and make things happen. And I wouldn't want to make a fuss, to no effect.

Besides, my children are having the vaccination. I'm taking the risk for the greater good, why can't everybody else?

And if I'm willing to risk my career (and children) for the greater good, then I must be a good person. And if I'm good, then it follows that anyone who opposes me is bad.

The mental gymnastics involved in trying to avoid doing your duty to your country, and your granny, are astounding and shameful.

I hope to have your vote in the next election, sailor.

Regards,

Rupert.

Monday 5 July 2021

Dear Rupert,

Thanks for taking the time to read this.

The Batley and Spen by-election was recently thrown away by the Conservative candidate, who lost by 323 votes.

The seat is around 20% Muslim and the major issues raised were the conflict between Israel and the Palestinians, and the disputed territory of Kashmir, claimed by both India and Pakistan.

Might the Conservatives have done better had they addressed more local concerns, such as the ruination of the life of the schoolteacher at Batley

Grammar School who showed a cartoon of the Prophet Muhammad? He broke no laws, followed the curriculum of his school, and is now in hiding with his family.

To have campaigned on free speech and the backwardness of tacit blasphemy laws may upset some of those who live in Batley, whose loyalties lie away from the values of this country, but may have encouraged others to come out and vote in favour of British norms and customs.

323 votes.

These issues seem distant in this part of the country but, as they get closer and closer, we may feel it might have paid to have dealt with them sooner - while they were manageable.

Yours sincerely,
Dan

Nothing From Rupert! Maybe he would have said this….

Dear Dan,

Holy smokes! Don't you have a day job? Batley-and-Spen sounds like a made up place name but, on the off chance that it is real, I will address your concerns.

We lost, okay? 323 is a lot of votes. Imagine 323 people, that's a lot. If they're all overweight, it's even more.

Speaking of size, India and Pakistan are huge. Should we just ignore them and hide our heads in the sand?

This thing about cartoons of the Prophet….I haven't seen one yet that has made me laugh. Not one! Given that this is the primary goal of a cartoon, then I think we're arguing over a failed enterprise.
Don't forget about hurt feelings, too. Our Government is basing all it's forthcoming legislation around the the dangers incurred by hurt feelings and I should remind you that no-one has feelings as tender and protected as a muslim. Well, a male muslim, anyway. Well, a straight, male muslim. Those guys………they've got the whole world against them! And such children too - they really need our protection.

I want to reassure you, I really do. Please use the enclosed form to tell me what protected characteristics you have, and what identity you identify with, and I'll send you the appropriate soothing message.

All my love,

Rupert.

Monday 12 July 2021

Dear Rupert,

Thanks for taking the time to read this.

The Scottish Hate Crime Bill, brought forward by SNP Justice Minister Humza Yousaf (a proponent of racist speech, see https://www.youtube.com/watch?v=BQ28yh7F228) instals protected characteristics, demolishes equality before the law, and criminalises conversations in private homes. It is sick, leads to division, self-censorship and is basically a creeping version of the thought police.

The (unelected) Law Commission has published a 553 page consultation that wants England and Wales to follow Scotland into authoritarianism.

The Commission wants to scrap satire and seeks to police publications.

It wants to multiply protected categories of person, fatally undermining equality under the law.

It wants to extend the boundaries of 'Hate Crime'. This when there were 120,000 'non-crime hate incidents' in the last 5 years: a crazy use of police time.

The Commission wants to protect 'philosophical belief'. This gives carte blanche to professional offence-takers (and renders those beliefs weak and 'threatened' by enquiry).

The Commission says that 'The whole point of hate-crime law….is to educate the public.' This is a zealot's language, where generally popular standards enforced by law morph into the law enforcing arbitrary ideological standards believed by a few.

The law has no jurisdiction inside the mind of a citizen. The law should be clear (is required to be so) and hate crime is incredibly subjective, as is 'philosophical belief'. The state's writ should not extend to the thoughts of an individual.

In Scotland, it is already at the dinner table of private homes.

Please vote against any future version of a hate-crime bill and any other measures which smuggle these principles into British life.

Yours sincerely,
Dan.

Rupert's Gone Missing! I'll Fill In For Him!

Dear Dan,

To state the vital, I hate hate crimes. Not hate in the sense of criminal hate, but everyday hate. Like the way you hate waking up before the butler has made that first Strawberry Daiquiri for your bedside table.

Still, any new law that reminds me that hate is wrong is a good law. I love to be educated, don't you? Oh! You already said you didn't…..but, listen, isn't it better to police yourself, rather than having the police do it? Those clever Scots! They know how to save a penny or two.
Reminds me of a funny joke: There's an Englishman, Irishman and a Scotsman…….um, wait. I shouldn't be thinking these things so close to the West Lothian Question. Oh, Lord, stop these thoughts! Unclean! Unclean!

So…..there's an Englishman, Englishman and another Englishman……

(Thank God there's people you can actually think these things about!)

Yours,

Rupert

Wednesday 14 July 2021

Dear Rupert,

Thanks for taking the time to read this.

I see that in the vote on July 13th you voted to mandate vaccinations for care home workers and the Ayes had it, with your help.

This was an immense shift in the relationship between government and the people.

Producing proof of your health status is an invasion of privacy, a call for discrimination and a communist-inspired plea to the abstract idea of the 'greater good' at the expense of the very real individuals who make up society. Add to that the comically low threat of death via COVID-19, the still experimental vaccines (which have a frighteningly high instant of confirmed deaths reported) and the guaranteed fracturing of an already (unnecessarily) traumatised public into different levels of health aparthied, I've got to think that you did a bad days work on Tuesday.

It is strange, don't you think, that a decision of this magnitude is made by statutory instrument, rather than parliament passing a new Act?

And it is odd that MPs only had 90 minutes to discuss it in the commons.

Weird that the vote was so curiously named, so it seemed that a majority of MPs did not turn up and voted by proxy - did they even know what the vote was fundamentally for (an MP present actually raised this question)?

A full impact assessment has been prepared, ministers were told….but no-one had seen it ahead of the vote, and its existence is still in question.

Still, it's only an untested vaccine.

And it's only the right to have control over one's own body.

And it's only the right to work.

And it's only the equal rights of citizens.

And it's only going to be care workers and nobody else, ever.

So, all alright then.

Yours sincerely,
Dan.

No Reply. Maybe It Would Have been Something Like This.

Dear Dan,

Every time I say black, you say white!   I mean, are you ever going to write a letter that just says, "Well Done!"?

Although, yes, I did vote by proxy, I assure you that I know exactly what the vote was for and so did all my MP friends, as we all advised each other.

I admit, there can be unforeseen consequences from voting. I mean, I don't have to tell you! I didn't expect a Conservative Government to lock down the country or enforce vaccine mandates or to Build Back Better, but there it is! Sometimes you have to hold on and enjoy the ride….and accept there is no-one else to vote for!

You've done it and I've done it. What's the difference between us except for my pay rise and privileges?

Yours ever-so-testily,
Rupert

Wednesday 21 July 2021

Dear Rupert,

Thanks for taking the time to read this.

On the 14th of July, I wrote to express how sickened I was by your proxy vote for mandated vaccines in care homes and how sure I was that this was the thin end of the wedge.

Five days later - five! - the Prime Minister announced that a vaccine passport was to be introduced for the long journey between the pavement and Britain's nightclubs. Announced on Freedom Day, no less. What a laugh he must have had.

Here are some uncontested facts.

1) Those double-jabbed-vaccinated still spread infection and can still catch Covid. They present just as much 'risk' as the unvaccinated.

2) The vaccine has not returned the country to normal life, as promised, after all the sacrifice of the last 16 months.

3) The average age of death from Covid is 82. One year older than the average life expectancy of a UK resident.

4) The young are at a statistically negligible risk of dying from Covid-19.

5) There is a cheap, tested alternative to the vaccine which has been used for decades. Of the billions who have taken it, only 35 have died from adverse reactions. In contrast to Ivermectin, the Covid vaccine deaths already measure in the thousands.

There's no justification for internal vaccine certification if any one of the five facts above are true.

Do you think they are untrue?

What is your justification for shredding the rights of care workers one day and young adults the next? Can you guarantee it'll be no-one else?

Do you disagree with coercion and perverse incentives to encourage good health, do you think it better to provide a cost/benefit analysis and let people choose?

Do you think the state has any business policing the private lives of citizens?

You might want to formulate some answers to these questions, because there will surely be a reckoning at some point. With the current uniformity of the political class over Covid, it worries me that that reckoning might not be at the ballot box.

**Yours sincerely,
Dan.**

No Reply. Here's Mine.

Dear Dan,
Ooooohhhhhhhhh. I don't think I can take much more of these letters, especially when they come in one after the other like this!
This is an emergency. EVERYBODY SAYS SO! Just get with the program! All the points you bring up are all very well but if we were to follow up each one then we would turn around and this emergency would be over…which would be fine if we could claim to have solved it! However, we must be seen to act, AND ACT WE WILL! IN UPPER-CASE IF NECESSARY BECAUSE IT'S THAT IMPORTANT!

With love,

Rupert.

Thursday 29 July 2021

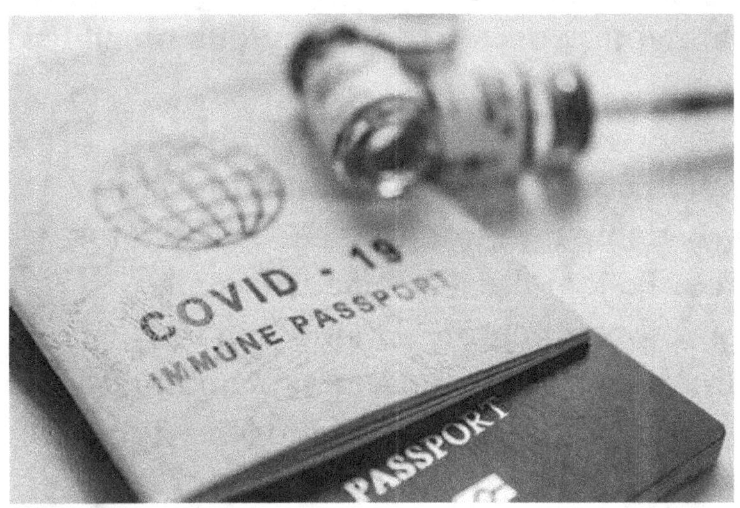

Dear Rupert,

Thanks for taking the time to read this.

I am writing about vaccine passports/certification.

'I have raised concerns about the proposals domestically and the UK Government have decided not to introduce these proposals. I was concerned about creating a tiered system of those who were vaccinated and those who were not yet vaccinated, as well as putting additional pressure on establishments to screen for these certifications also, as many businesses are already following strict social distancing and public health guidance in order to be able to trade.'

These were your words from a previous email to me.

Your name is conspicuously absent from the cross-party campaign to oppose COVID-status certificates. To join the list, please e-mail info@bigbrotherwatch.org.uk and join the parliamentarians (43 Conservatives amongst them) who are prepared to stand for the rights and values that others have died for. At bigbrotherwatch.org.uk there are a list of reasons to do so, should you need them.

Vote against Vaccine Passports, sir. It'll be too late, after the fact.

This is a blood-on-the-streets matter and if you are going to quietly acquiesce or fight for passports on their merits I would be grateful to know and understand your reasoning. It would be a massive relief to be convinced that I am wrong on this matter.

It is customary now to have to (pathetically) explain that I am not an anti-vaxxer. I do not object to people taking the covid vaccine, with informed consent. I object to fear-mongering and I object to having to wear a Star of David. The

idea that you can tell my kids to do the same is beyond the pale.

The average age of death from COVID is 82.

Life expectancy in the UK is 81.

**Yours sincerely,
Dan.**

No Reply. Here's Mine.

Dear Danny boy,
Big old sigh……..
Using my old words against me, eh? Classic gambit but you forgot that you were dealing with a politician, didn't you? I love listening to myself speak, whether I am right, wrong or moronic.
I do agree that vaccine passports are discriminatory and wrong. Still, on balance, they cause me very little bother and allow me to go on my annual holiday, which I like to take three times a year.
Incidentally, if you are trying to get me to revoke passports by scaring me with violence at home, then think again. If I don't have a vaccine passport, how the hell could I get out of the country, to safety?

Try to think through your logic a little better next time, old fellow.

Rupert.

Monday 30 August 2021

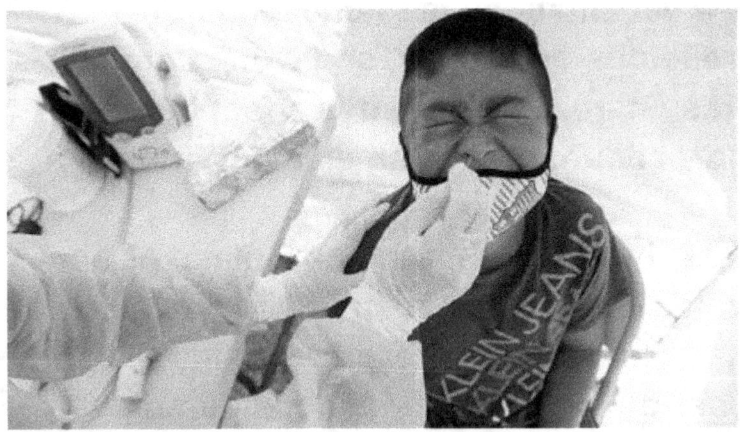

Dear Rupert,

Thanks for taking the time to read this.

An NHS plan has recently come to light (via a Telegraph whistleblower) to make room in schools for the vaccination of 12 year-olds by newly recruited staff, in time for the new school term.
Also included in this plan is a reduction in the waiting time for parental consent. It has been reduced from 2 weeks to 48 hours.

**Children who are assessed to be Gillick Competent will be able to take the vaccination without their parent's consent. The parents do not even need to be informed. Parents of a 12 year old.

To enter into a rant about the efficacy and safety of the new vaccinations is to challenge the current religious orthodoxy, so I won't commit such heresy here. However, it is a fact that any medical procedure carries an element of risk.

. I would ask, in the case of the new plans of the hallowed NHS, where the responsibility would lie in the case of an adverse reaction inside the body of a 12 year-old child who was considered capable of consent to a vaccination (though not able to drink, smoke etc).

Would responsibility lie with those carrying out the vaccination? They, surely, would have to properly explain the costs and benefits, in addition to establishing competency.

Would responsibility lie with the drug manufacturer?

Would the responsibility lie with the child?

Or would the responsibility lie with the child's parents? Who, without forewarning, would suddenly be responsible in every other way:

caring for a child who may be permanently harmed, disabled and traumatised. Or, in the extreme cases, left grieving for a child. A child who, in every other way except for a Covid Vaccination, remains their responsibility, by law.

What a bloody disgrace, that any Government, any health service, any school, can consider this.

Average age of death from COVID 19 is (still) above the average age of life expectancy in the UK. And the US. And in Europe.

Yours sincerely,
Dan.

No Reply - Try This.

Dear Dan,

For the love of God, calm down!

I have children, don't you know, and if I am prepared to allow them Gillick competency - who makes these names up? - you should too.   Let's face it, based on your letters to me, I'm sure you'll agree that they are far more qualified to make decisions than I am. Can't answer that, can you? Blinded you with logic!

It's the right of every parent to ensure the right of
every child to have the right to ensure the right of
every granny to stay alive.
Answer that, facist!

Don't forget to vote at the local elections!

Love,

Rupert.

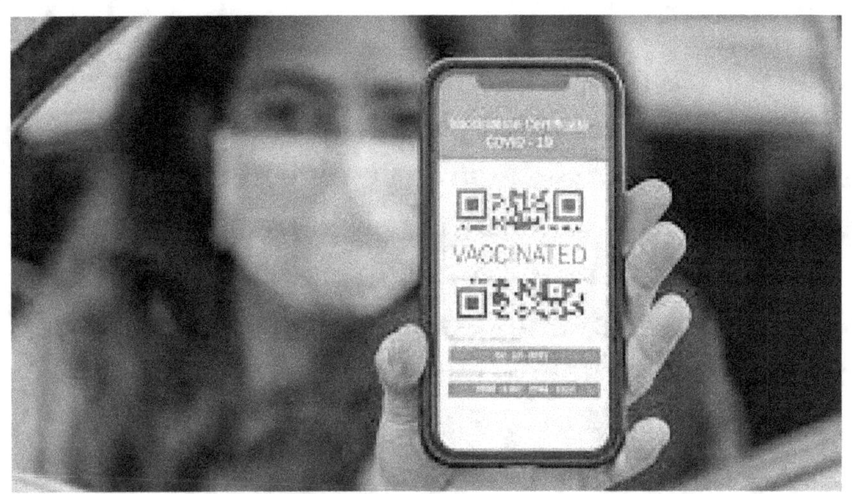

Tuesday 14 September 2021

Dear Rupert,

Thanks for taking the time to read this.

I am writing to ask you to vote against mandatory Covid Passes in any forthcoming Parliamentary votes.

Covid-19 vaccines are actually not standard vaccines and have not been proven safe, indeed they are more dangerous than all normal vaccines that have previously been introduced combined.

Covid-19 vaccines (I'll call them that under protest) protect the vaccinated from death, it seems, when they are already extremely ill , but data from the UK and other highly vaccinated countries now unequivocally show that none of the vaccines prevent you catching or transmitting Coronavirus, which would be the basis for introducing the Covid Pass.

The announcement that the Covid Pass would be introduced goes against the advice of the UK Parliament's Public Administration and Constitutional Affairs Committee report into Covid-19 status certification, which found that the government could not make a strong scientific case for vaccine passports, and that they would be discriminatory. The report was also clear that it is imperative the Government should produce a cost-benefit analysis, with full financial costings and detailed modelling of the potential impacts. The Government has failed to provide these for public scrutiny.

To summarise my concerns, I believe that

- the Covid Pass would be discriminatory on the grounds of race, religion and socio-economic status;

- the Covid Pass would be harmful to the economy as it is impractical for businesses to implement;

- there is no strong scientific justification for the unevidenced Covid Pass;

- the vast majority of the adult population have had two doses of a Covid-19 vaccine and, according to the Office of National Statistics, nine out of ten adults have antibodies to Covid-19, so any Covid Pass scheme introduced at this point would be costly, with only diminishing returns;

- the Government has not been transparent in its intentions. At the time when Parliamentary Under-Secretary of State for COVID-19 Vaccine Deployment of United Kingdom Nadhim Zahawi made assurances that there were no plans to introduce the Covid Pass, the Government had already issued eight contracts to develop one. Such lack of transparency is eroding trust in the Government and Parliament;

- the Covid Pass would damage informed consent. The Council of Europe resolution on Covid-19 vaccines details ethical, legal and practical considerations for ensuring a high vaccine uptake, and urges Member States to "ensure that citizens are informed that the vaccination is not mandatory and that no one is under political, social or other pressure to be vaccinated if they do not wish to do so; ensure that no one is discriminated against for not having been vaccinated, due to possible health risks or not wanting to be vaccinated";

- the Covid Pass might actually be counter-productive, as reported by the All-Party Parliamentary Group on Vaccines for All, and in a recent study published by the MDPI entitled '"Vaccine Passports" May Backfire: Findings from a cross-sectional study in the UK and Israel on willingness to get vaccinated against COVID-19'. This could affect faith in future public health initiatives;

- the Covid Pass would create an illiberal medical papers-based checkpoint society that is completely out of keeping with our British way of life.

Furthermore, no impact assessment of the introduction of the Covid Pass has been made publicly available.

I am very concerned about the Covid Pass, and your decision to support the Government will affect my vote.

Overall life expectancy in the UK is still lower than the average age of death from Covid, though the lockdown driven NHS backlog may soon change this.

Yours sincerely,
Dan

Rupert, Where Are You?

Dear Dan,

That was a long one!

Naw, not doing that.

All the best!

Rupert.

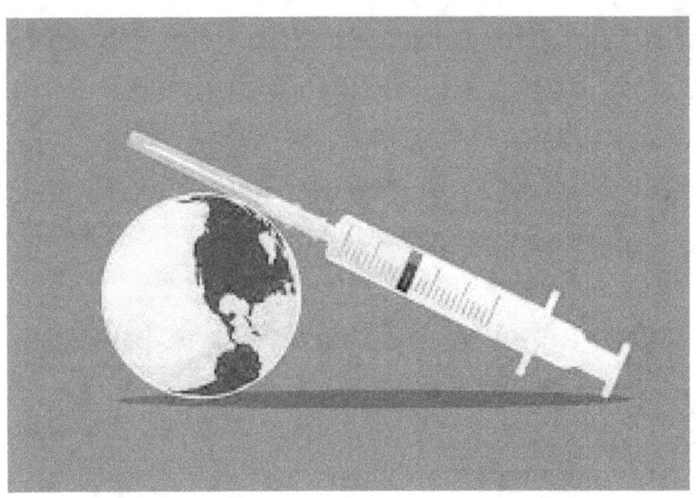

Monday 20 September 2021

Dear Rupert,

Thanks for taking the time to read this.

The subject of Covid vaccinations for children is due to be debated on Tuesday September 21, at 9:30am, in Westminster Hall. Can I ask you to attend and speak against them?

My instinct is that your answer is no. If I am wrong in that supposition, I sincerely apologise.

The JCVI's (Joint Committee on Vaccination and Immunisation) recently dismissed report clearly shows that no healthy children died from Covid-19 in the period February 2020 to March 2021. (https://www.gov.uk/government/news/jcvi-issues-updated-advice-on-covid-19-vaccination-of-children-aged-12-to-15).

The Committee has advised the Government that children of this age range should not be vaccinated.

As you know, the Government has ignored this and is pressing ahead, citing the greater good, as all good totalitarians do.

The JCVI have previously recommended the rollout of vaccines to 16-17 year olds (an equally indefensible proposition). Since then, they have been notified of their liability, under national and international law, by lawyers working unpaid and, truly, for the greater good (https://www.bitchute.com/video/Ku3Abhtq10Dy/).

Is it a coincidence that this time around they have recommended a saner route, where, should the worst come to the worst, they will not be held accountable for deaths or injury caused?

If I were to read in a newspaper that a child had gone to school, undergone a medical treatment

without informed consent
(https://www.conservativewoman.co.uk/the-utter-shambles-of-child-covid-vaccine-consent/), without the consent of the parents (https://www.conservativewoman.co.uk/parents-prepare-if-you-want-to-protect-your-child-from-the-states-needle/) and without direct health benefits for the child and that child died, then I would consider that a crime had taken place and I think there would be general agreement on that.

History has shown that the persons responsible would not be able to claim ignorance and would feel the full weight of the law as applied for murder or manslaughter. It is important that those just doing their job (from MPs, to nurses, to teachers) are aware that their day's work could lead to such an end.

Doctors For Covid Ethics (https://doctors4covidethics.medium.com/) is a group of doctors and scientists from 30 countries who have served all the members of the European Parliament with a notice of liability, similar to that served to the JCVI. They have all now been made aware of the dangers of following party lines and using that as cover for individual actions: i.e. there is no cover.

Here in the UK, an open letter was sent to Professor Chris Whitty and his counterparts in the devolved parliaments. The letter was signed by 60 UK doctors and can be found here: https://www.conservativewoman.co.uk/sixty-doctors-plead-with-chief-medical-officers-to-reject-child-vaccination/
The letter, like many others sent to the government, warns of the dangers of unnecessarily vaccinating those children who we are put here to protect.

The arguments are clearly before you and your fellow MP's. The debate is tomorrow at 9:30.

Life expectancy in the UK is 81 years. The average age of death with Covid is now over 83.

Don't risk our kids for this.

Yours sincerely,
Dan

I Think Rupert's Given Up On Me.

Dear Dan,

This is one of your veiled threat letters, don't think I can't see them coming by now.

I am getting sorely tempted to dress up as the devil and turn up at your house with a hyperdeemic nerdle and a Government mandate. But I won't.

Look, I have no power. Zero. I'm not Bill Gates. I'm not Klaus Schwab. I'm not George Soros. Boris Johnson has to carry their lunch at WEF meetings, and I have to carry Boris'.

What exactly do you want from me? All I want is to get through life with as little trouble, responsibility and time with my wife as possible. That's precisely why I became an MP. I was assured a mistress too, so you're not the only one who was lied to by a Cabinet Minister.

Yours,

Rupert.

Friday 8 October 2021

Dear Rupert,

Thanks for taking the time to read this.

On Tuesday 5th October there was a vote in the Senedd.

Tory MS Gareth Davies failed to vote, despite clearly having the opportunity to do so. His excuse of a failed zoom call is dismal at best as he could easily have voted by phone.Now we have Vaxx passports in Wales, entirely due to him.

What action is going to be taken here? Why did the Tory opposition group not call for a standing order to abandon the vote for a later date?

Do all the Welsh parliament secretly want Vaccine passports? That's the assumption I have after this lousy, pathetic display.

How can voters have any confidence in government when it is conducted like this? For nearly two years we have been governed by diktat. Now, we're back to voting and it's the same thing in all but name. Something stinks, doesn't it?

Yours sincerely,

Dan.

Nada. Here's Mine.

Dear Dan,

They got me a mistress!!!!

Oh, happy day!!!

Thought you'd like to know!!!!

God bless!!!!!

Love, love, love,

Rupert.

Wednesday 10 November 2021

Dear Rupert,

Thanks for taking the time to read this.

A new report (https://www.oecd-ilibrary.org/social-issues-migration-health/health-at-a-glance_19991312) from the OECD has shown that the pandemic took life expectancy in the UK in 2020 back to 2010 levels. Life expectancy at birth dropped by one year from 81.4 to 80.4, a level last seen in 2009. In 2008 it was even lower at 79.8.

This is terrible and must be blamed on the deadly virus Covid-19, which has a survival rate of over 99% and an average age of death of 83. It clearly has nothing to do with the collateral damage from shutting down the country and prioritising Covid above all other illnesses.

I would say, however, that there is no need to panic. I remember 2010. It wasn't so bad. Maybe we were braver then.

Lockdowns, masks, distancing, vaccination mandates. No doubt about it, we were braver then.

Yours sincerely,

Dan.

My MP Replied

Dear Dan,

Thank you for contacting me about the Health and Care Bill which is currently going through Parliament. As I am sure you are aware, healthcare reform is a very emotive issue and I think it is important that we have a serious discussion about what steps we take to reform the health and social care system in the UK and I look forward to taking the views of my constituents to Parliament.

I completely agree with you that the unprecedented threat of the COVID-19 pandemic reminded us how vital our health and care system is to all of us. I want to assure you that the NHS will always be free at the point of use, and any proposed reforms will aim to continue to improve the quality of these services and patient outcomes. The NHS will always remain under public ownership, and while private companies have formed a part of the healthcare system since the early 2000's, they will not own assets, or direct healthcare policy.

As we recover from this pandemic, it is right and necessary that our health and care services are at the forefront. The pandemic underlies not only the dedication and skill of those in this sector, but also the necessity of a broader, more integrated health and care system. I welcome the intention to develop more integrated care between the NHS, Local Government and other partners including the voluntary and community sector, which will be vital in tackling the factors that affect the long-term sustainability of patient services. The Bill will make permanent some of the innovations brought about by the pandemic. I understand that these proposed reforms will also include proper accountability mechanisms and give patients and the public the confidence that they are receiving the best care from their healthcare system.

The measures set out in the Health and Care Bill deliver on the NHS's own proposals for reform in its Long Term Plan. I believe these proposals have been developed in consultation with key stakeholders in this sector, and I am encouraged by the preliminary positive feedback received. In particular, the comments from the former Chief Executive of NHS England, who said that this Bill *"will support our health and care services to be more integrated and innovative so the NHS can thrive in the decades to come", are reassuring.*

Thank you again for taking the time to contact me. While healthcare is devolved to the Welsh Government, I know many *********** residents travel into England for their care, and this is why I will continue to take a keen interest in this Bill as it progresses through Parliament.**

With kind regards,

Rupert.

My Reaction

Is it me……..is this a reply to…..somebody else's letter?
HOLY CRAP! WHAT A GREAT WAY TO END THE YEAR!
The system works.